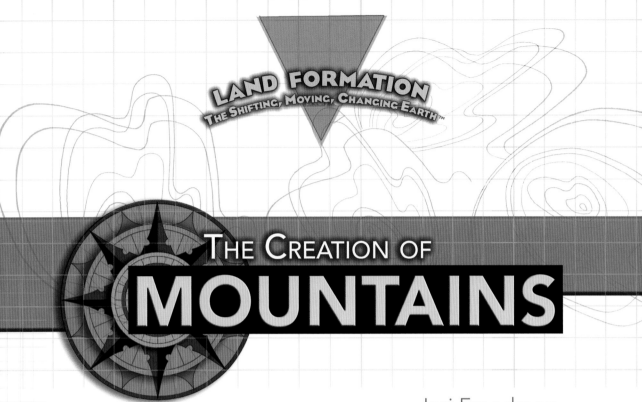

LAND FORMATION
THE SHIFTING, MOVING, CHANGING EARTH™

THE CREATION OF
MOUNTAINS

Jeri Freedman

rosen publishing's
rosen
central®

New York

To my mother, Delores Jardine, who shared her love of geology with me

Published in 2010 by The Rosen Publishing Group, Inc.
29 East 21st Street, New York, NY 10010

First Edition

Library of Congress Cataloging-in-Publication Data

Freedman, Jeri.
The creation of mountains / Jeri Freedman.—1st ed.
    p. cm.—(Land formation: the shifting, moving, changing earth)
Includes bibliographical references and index.
ISBN-13: 978-1-4358-5300-3 (library binding)
ISBN-13: 978-1-4358-5598-4 (pbk)
ISBN-13: 978-1-4358-5599-1 (6-pack)
1. Mountains—Juvenile literature. 2. Landscape changes—Juvenile literature. 3. Mountain ecology—Juvenile literature. I. Title.
GB512.F74 2010
551.43'2—dc22

                                                    2008044014

Manufactured in Malaysia

On the cover: The Sierra Nevada mountains in California.

CONTENTS

INTRODUCTION

About 4.5 billion years ago, our sun and its surrounding solar system began to form from a chaotically rotating cloud of dust and gas. Tiny particles of oxygen and minerals (such as iron and silicon), ice, and other elements clumped together to form the early earth. In the centuries that followed, the primitive earth was bombarded by meteorites (chunks of rock from outer space).

At first, because of the heat generated by the collisions that formed the planet, it remained molten (in a melted state). As it cooled, the surface of the earth became solid, but the core remained molten and metal-rich. As the newly created planet experienced centuries of violent weather and geologic events, such as volcanic eruptions, it developed the basic geologic features we see today. However, the distribution of geologic structures like mountains, lakes, oceans, and other surface features differed from what we see today.

Mountains play a key role in the earth's current environment and will continue to do so in the future. They affect wind flow and climate, including temperature and rainfall, provide a home for people and animals, and supply useful metals and minerals.

Mountains not only provide majestic scenery but affect the climate of the surrounding land.

But just what is a mountain? In general, a mountain can be considered any landmass that projects above the surrounding surface of the land. Most experts feel that a landmass should have a peak in order to be considered a mountain. One thing there is no agreement about, however, is how high a rising projection needs to be before it can be called a mountain.

Some expert sources consider a mountain to be 200 feet (61 meters) to 3,280 feet (1,000 m) above the surrounding land; others don't specify any particular height. Mountains cover about 25 percent of the earth's land area.

Scientists have developed a number of tools to study the formation of geologic structures like mountains. Studying such structures allows us to learn how the earth has changed and evolved. It helps us understand the forces that change the physical structures of the earth and predict what changes might take place in the future.

CHAPTER 1

WHAT ARE MOUNTAINS?: EARLY STUDIES

A mountain range is a chain of mountains. It is separated from other ranges by low-lying areas of land (valleys) and other natural elements, such as rivers, making it a distinct entity. The highest mountain range in the world is the Himalayas, located in Asia. The Himalayas cover a band that crosses India, Nepal, Tibet, Bhutan, and part of China. They include many mountains more than 23,500 feet (7,150 m) high. The longest mountain range on any continent is the Andes, located along the western coast of South America. They are 4,400 miles (7,000 kilometers) long.

There are mountain ranges on every continent. Some well-known mountain ranges include the Himalayas in Asia; the Ural Mountains in western Russia; the Alps in Europe; the Balkan and Carpathian mountains in eastern Europe; the Caucasus Mountains in Russia, Georgia, Azerbaijan, and Armenia; the Cotswolds in southwestern England; the Andes and Sierra Madres in South America; the Pyrenees in France and Spain; and the Appalachian, Ozark, Cascade, and Rocky mountains in North America. Altogether, there are more than a hundred mountain ranges around the world.

Mountain ranges are often subdivided

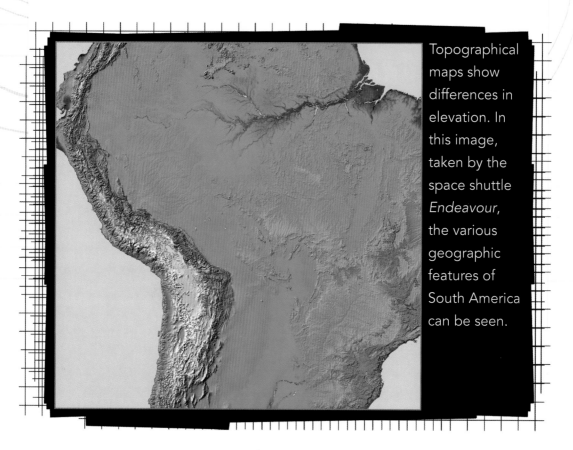

Topographical maps show differences in elevation. In this image, taken by the space shuttle *Endeavour*, the various geographic features of South America can be seen.

into subranges located in specific areas. For example, the White Mountains in New Hampshire and the Green Mountains in Vermont are part of the Appalachian Mountains.

Land isn't the only place that mountains exist. In fact, the longest mountain range in the world is actually located under the Atlantic Ocean. It is called the Mid-Atlantic Ridge. It is C-shaped and is located in the area between South America and Africa. However, it is not the only underwater mountain range. Underwater ridges are found in oceans all over the world. Underwater mountains are sometimes called seamounts.

THE WORLD'S HIGHEST MOUNTAINS

Where are the world's highest mountains? The highest mountain is Mauna Kea. It is located on the island of Hawaii. It rises only 13,796 feet (4,205 m) above sea level. Mauna Kea rises not from land but from the floor of the Pacific Ocean. It is actually 33,476 feet (10,203 m) high. The second tallest mountain? It is Mount Everest, which is located in the Himalayas. It is 29,035 feet (8,850 m) tall. As a matter of fact, ten of the top twelve highest mountains are located in the Himalayas. The exception, other than Mauna Kea, is K2, located in the Karakoram Range, in Pakistan and China. It is the next highest mountain after Mount Everest and rises 28,250 feet (8,611 m). Listed here are the tallest mountains on each continent:

Continent	Mountain	Range	Feet	Meters
Africa	Kilimanjaro	None	19,340	5,895
Antarctica	Vinson Massif	Sentinel Range (Ellsworth Mtns.)	16,066	4,897
Asia	Mount Everest	Himalayas	29,035	8,850
Australia	Mount Kosciusko	Snowy Mountains	7,310	2,228
Europe	Elbrus	Caucasus Mountains (Russia)	18,510	5,642
North America	Mount McKinley (also called Denali)	Alaska Range (Alaska)	20,230	6,194
South America	Aconcagua	Andes (Argentina)	22,834	6,960

Early Theories About How Mountains Were Formed

One of the earliest scientific theories of how mountains were produced was proposed in 1544 by the German scientist Georg Bauer (1494–1555), who wrote under the Latin version of his name, Georgius Agricola. (*Bauer* is German for "farmer," and *Agricola* is Latin for the same word.) After spending a great deal of time studying the rock and mineral formations in the vicinity of a German mining town, he wrote *De ortu et causis subterraneorum* (*On the Origin and Causes of Underground Phenomena*). His book is considered the first major work on mineralogy. Agricola proposed that mountains were formed by a combination of natural processes. These included erosion by water and earthquakes.

In 1659, Nicholas Steno (1639–1686), a student at the University of Copenhagen, applied the study of geometry to the concept of mountain building. In a notebook he wrote, he suggested that mountains could have been created by the upthrusting, slippage, or falling of the earth's strata, or layers.

In the nineteenth century, it was generally believed that mountains were formed because the outer surface of the molten core of earth had gradually solidified. In 1827, Louis Cordier (1777–1861), professor of geology at the Museum of Natural History in Paris, established that the temperature of the earth's crust decreases closer to the surface. He did this by measuring the temperature of the crust at various depths. In the process, he showed that the temperature changed in a gradual pattern called a gradient. Geologists at the time associated the temperature gradient with the gradual cooling of the earth. The common

Jean-Baptiste Elie de Beaumont's theory of mountain creation was incorrect. However, his research contributed greatly to geologists' knowledge of the structure of mountains.

belief was that as the earth cooled, it contracted and its surface developed folds, much as a grape develops folds as it dries and becomes a raisin. They believed that this folding process resulted in the mountains.

In 1852, French geologist Jean-Baptiste Elie de Beaumont (1798–1874) developed a new theory called the Jaws of a Vise to explain mountain building. He proposed that in some places, mountains were created by a process in which the land was crushed and folded, as if caught in the jaws of a giant vise. He suggested that this force was the result of large masses of rock thrusting into each other. His focus was on the vertical movement

Pangaea was the supercontinent that formed approximately 300 million years ago. It broke up about 200 million years ago, eventually forming today's continents.

of landmasses against each other, pushing land up to form mountains.

Eduard Suess (1831–1914), a geologist and professor at the University of Vienna, studied the Alps. He proposed that the Mediterranean Sea is all that remains of a once vast ocean, and that the Alps were once at the bottom of that ancient sea. He also theorized that Africa, India, and South America were once one continent that had separated. The mechanisms he proposed for mountain building and changes in landmasses were not completely correct. However, he was the first to recognize the importance of horizontal movement of landmasses in creating mountains.

In 1910, German meteorologist (a scientist who studies climate) Alfred Wegener (1880–1930) proposed that the earth had once contained a single giant continent, which he called Pangaea. He suggested that a tendency of landmasses to drift apart was responsible for Pangaea breaking up into multiple smaller continents that moved around the surface of the earth. He called this process continental drift. The scientific community of his day strongly rejected his theory. However, subsequently discovered evidence from the distribution of rocks and fossils (the remains of prehistoric plants and animals that have turned to stone) has been found to support this theory.

VISUALIZING THE GEOLOGIC PAST

Many changes happen to mountains over millions of years. They form, break down and disappear, and arise again. A major area of study for geologists is figuring out what the composition of mountains was at different periods of the earth's history. This information on the makeup of mountains at different periods gives us an idea what the earth was like in the distant past and on the forces that cause it to change.

The study of the earth is called geology, and scientists who study the earth are called geologists. There are two major areas of geology: historical geology and physical geology. Historical geology studies when significant events in the earth's formation and history occurred, such as when the original landmass of the planet separated into individual continents. Physical geology studies the physical forces, such as mountain building, that work on the earth and the components that make up the earth, including rocks and minerals.

Studying Rock Strata

Different types of rocks occur in layers called strata. By examining the composition of rocks in different strata, scientists can

You can clearly see the different strata in the mountains of Alberta, Canada, indicated by the different-colored bands of rock.

learn about what the earth was like in various time periods. In geology, strata are layers of rock that have characteristics that are distinct from those of the other layers around them.

These layers are usually piled on top of each other like layers in a layer cake. They were produced over many millions of years by natural forces that caused different types of material to be deposited. For example, layers could be made up of sandstone (sand-based rock), coal-based material, lava, and so on. Strata can extend over vast distances. Strata are often visible in cliff walls and highway cut-throughs as bands of different-colored rock.

Rocks and Minerals That Compose Mountains

Elements are the most basic materials. The earth's crust is made mainly of eight elements. The most common elements in the crust are silicon and oxygen. The six other elements are aluminum, iron, calcium, magnesium, sodium, and potassium. These elements combine to form minerals that compose the features of the earth's surface, including mountains.

Minerals combine to form rocks. In general, rocks are divided into various types based on their composition. The major categories of rocks include the following.

Igneous Rocks

Igneous rocks are formed from molten rock, called magma. The molten rock can come from the earth's mantle or crust. Often, igneous rocks are formed by the remelting of previously existing rock. They make up the majority of rock in the earth's crust, but they

GEOLOGIC EONS

Since the earth dates back billions of years, geologists deal with enormous periods of time. In the nineteenth century, geologists showed that all around the world rock strata followed the same sequence in time. They used evidence such as fossilized plants and animals to verify this. This allowed them to form a continuous geologic timeline. They called this timeline the geologic column.

Geologists divided the billions of years of the earth's existence into four major divisions called eons: the Hadean, Archean, Proterozoic, and Phanerozoic. Because there exists an enormous amount of fossils from the Phanerozoic eon, which is the most recent, geologists are able to date strata from that eon more precisely. Therefore, they divided the Phanerozoic into three shorter spans called eras: the Paleozoic era, Mesozoic era, and Cenozoic era. They then divided eras into smaller divisions called periods, such as the Jurassic period, which covered tens of millions of years. Finally, they divided periods into smaller divisions called epochs, such as the Pleistocene epoch. Later, the epochs were further subdivided into ages, covering millions of years. In 2004, for the first time in 130 years, the International Union of Geological Sciences recognized a new period: the Ediacaran period in the Neoproterozoic era.

This fossil palm shows that the land was once subtropical and low-lying in contrast to its elevation today.

Cross-bedding is the creation of narrow lines in rock faces by changes in the direction of wind currents.

are often covered by a layer of sedimentary and metamorphic rocks. Examples of igneous rocks include granite and basalt.

Sedimentary Rocks

As their name suggests, sedimentary rocks are formed from sediments, particles that result from the weathering and erosion of rock. As sediment builds up, pressure compacts it into rocks. This process is called lithification. Sedimentary rocks form layers, or strata. They contain fossils, the remains of ancient plants and animals that have turned to stone. Because sedimentary rocks form distinct strata, they are very useful for dating purposes. Examples of sedimentary rocks are limestone, sandstone, and shale.

Metamorphic Rocks

Metamorphic rocks are formed when other types of rock are submitted to heat and pressure. This process causes a

metamorphosis, or change, in the rocks. The metamorphosis
may be the result of the collision of tectonic plates, or it may be
caused by the immense heat and pressure that come from
massive layers of rock above the affected rocks. The metamorphic process changes the nature of the rocks. For example,

shale is transformed into slate, and limestone is transformed into marble.

Dating Strata

One approach to dating strata is lithostratigraphy. This approach studies strata for changes in form that indicate changes from one stratum to another. Because we know what certain types of change mean in terms of the environment, we can gain information on what was going on environmentally in the location where a change in strata occurred. A related technique is chemostratigraphy. Chemostratigraphy is the measurement of tiny amounts of elements, such as carbon and oxygen, in different strata. Changes in the amounts of elements in the strata provide information on changes that were taking place in the environment at different periods.

Another approach to dating strata is biostratigraphy. In this process, scientists examine the fossilized plants and animals that are found in the strata and date the rock according to when those plants and animals were known to have lived. This method was originally developed in the nineteenth century. It was the primary method of dating strata until the development of high-technology methods, such as radiometry, in the twentieth century.

Geochronology

Using techniques to date strata directly is called geochronology. Radiometry relies on naturally occurring elements that are radio-active. These elements give off radiation that decreases over time. Each element takes a certain time to give off all its radiation, or decay. By measuring how much radiation the element is still giving off, or emitting, scientists can tell how old the rock that contains it is.

A type of radiometric dating that you may have heard of is radiocarbon dating. This approach measures the amount of radiation given off by a form of the element carbon, called carbon-14. However, radiocarbon dating can only be used to date rocks that are 50,000 years old or less. There are a number of other radiometric dating methods. Two that are useful for dating older rocks are uranium-thorium dating and uranium-lead dating. Uranium-thorium dating is used to measure the age of fossils, bones, corals, and similar materials. It can date objects up to 700,000 years old. Uranium-lead dating is used to measure the age of rocks greater than one million years old. Radiometric dating is not the only way to measure the age of rocks, however.

For dating minerals like quartz and feldspar, which are crystals, geologists use luminescence techniques ("luminescence" refers to light). Crystals have regular internal structures that can trap atomic particles called electrons. There are a variety of luminescence techniques, but they all basically rely on stimulating the electrons trapped in the crystal structure. This causes the electrons to give off energy in the form of light, which can be measured by a detector.

The metal-rich core of the earth creates a magnetic field as the planet spins. This magnetic field is what causes the needle on a compass to point toward the North Pole. The strength and direction of the magnetic field of the earth has changed from time to time. Scientists can tell how old a stratum is by finding out the strength and direction of the magnetic field at the time the stratum was formed. To do this, they use a geochronological

One approach to dating rocks is chiseling out a block of sediment for luminescence dating, such as from this ancient dune in South Africa.

technique called magnetostigraphy. They can do this because, as fine metal particles pass through water, they line up with the direction of the magnetic field. The amount of magnetism and the direction of the field present at the time the metal particles become part of the surrounding rock are frozen and never change.

Scientists also collect samples from strata. They then analyze the samples using a technique called natural remnant magnetization. In this technique, the normal permanent level of magnetization found in rock is subtracted from that of the sample to arrive at the remaining level of magnetization. The amount of magnetization is then compared to a standard table that shows the level of magnetization at different time periods to establish the age of the strata.

THE GEOLOGIC STRUCTURE OF THE EARTH

The earth is composed of three major layers. At the center is the core. It has two parts. The part at the center is called the inner core. It is a solid ball, most likely composed mainly of iron and nickel. It is about 1,516 miles (2,440 km) in diameter. The temperature at the core is about 6,692 degrees Fahrenheit (3,700 degrees Celsius). The reason that it is solid at that temperature, instead of melted, is that the pressure at the center of the earth is so great that it compresses the material into a solid ball.

Around the inner core is a layer about 1,800 miles (2,900 km) thick. This is the outer core. It is composed mainly of a molten mix of iron and nickel. Around the outer core is a layer made of rock. It is called the mantle. The mantle has two parts. The uppermost part of the mantle, where it meets the crust, is firm. But lower down, the mantle is hot and solid but soft, like taffy. The outermost layer is the crust, which is solid rock. On land, the crust is composed mainly of granite and is 30–40 miles (45–64 km) thick. This type of crust is called continental crust. It is thickest under mountains. Under the ocean is the oceanic crust, which is only 4–5 miles

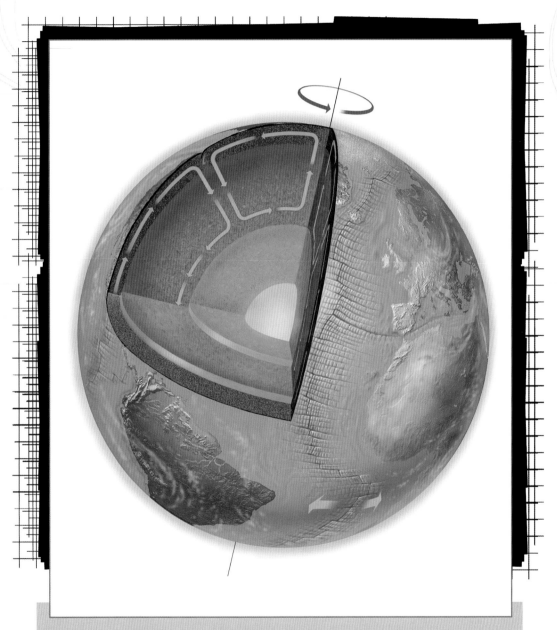

The tectonic plates (outer layer) float on the semiliquid mantle (orange layer). Convection in the mantle, caused by heat rising from the core (yellow), causes the plates to move.

(6–8 km) thick. The major component of oceanic crust is basalt. Because the material that makes up oceanic crust is denser than that of continental crust, oceanic crust is usually below sea level (the average level of the sea between high and low tides), whereas continental crust generally rises above sea level. The solid part of the earth—the crust and the upper rocky layer of the mantle—is called the lithosphere ("litho" comes from *lithos*, the Greek word for "stone"). The area of the mantle below the lithosphere, which is semirigid, is called the asthenosphere (it gets its name from *asthenes*, the Greek word for "frail").

The Tectonic Plates and Mountain Building

Mountains can be created by the collisions of tectonic plates or volcanic eruption. Tectonic plates contribute to mountain building. In the 1960s, the theory was first proposed that tectonic plates play a key role in the physical evolution of the earth. "Tectonic" comes from the Greek word *tekton*, which means "mason" or "builder."

Tectonic plates are flat slabs on which the continents float. Scientific evidence discovered in the twentieth century demonstrated that the theories proposed in the nineteenth century about how mountains form were wrong. Those theories rested on the idea that the core of the earth is cooling and that this causes the crust of the earth to crinkle. In fact, the core of the earth is not cooling, and the surface is actually expanding rather than contracting. Current scientific thought is that as the

SATELLITES AND MOUNTAIN MAPPING

New technologies provide the ability to measure aspects of the earth in ways that were impossible in the past. One tool we did not have until the second half of the twentieth century is satellite imaging. With the advent of permanent satellites in space, it has become possible to view mountains in new ways. Satellites make it possible to gather data about mountains and create images of them in several ways. One approach is called radiometry. This technique uses sensors to measure radio waves, visible light, infrared light (light waves too short to be seen with the naked eye), or ultraviolet radiation (light waves too long to be viewed with the naked eye).

One type of radiometry is called passive radiometry. Passive radiometry uses sensors to measure the visible, infrared, or ultraviolet light that hits structures on the earth from natural sources and is reflected back from those structures. In active radiometry, radio waves are deliberately bounced off the surface of the earth, and the time it takes them to be bounced back to the sensor is measured. Measurements of the light or radio waves are collected by the sensors on the satellite. A computer then uses those measurements to make pictures of the structure being mapped. These pictures reveal important characteristics of surface structures, such as the features of mountains and the location of minerals.

Mountains are mapped by combining a group of high-altitude images taken by the U.S. Geological Survey.

27

Ravines and cliffs mark the place where the North American and European tectonic plates meet near Pingvellir, Iceland. Continental drift is moving the plates apart.

tectonic plates move and landmasses collide, mountains are formed. And when they move apart and landmasses are stretched, valleys form. The major tectonic plates are the African Plate, Antarctic Plate, Australian Plate, Eurasian Plate, North American Plate, South American Plate, and Pacific Plate.

Except for the Pacific Plate, which is an oceanic plate under the Pacific Ocean, all of these are continental plates. However, tectonic plates often contain some oceanic crust along their edges. In addition to the major tectonic plates, there are a number of smaller plates scattered around the world.

Motion of Tectonic Plates

Tectonic plates are described by their edges. When two plates move toward each other, the result is convergent margins. In this case, the edges of two plates converge, or meet. If two landmasses meet, the result is a continent-continent margin. If two ocean

plates meet, the result is an ocean-ocean margin. If a continent and an ocean meet, the result is a continent-ocean margin. When an ocean plate converges with a continental plate, subduction occurs. Subduction is the sinking of the ocean plate beneath another plate. Locations where subduction occurs are called subduction zones. Sometimes when tectonic plates converge, they crash together. In this case, their edges crumple up just like the metal of two cars that collide. The result is the creation of mountain ranges. The area where the contact occurs is called a collision zone.

Tectonic plates can move away from each other as well as toward each other. When this occurs, the margins are called divergent margins. The process of pulling apart is often violent and marked by the occurrence of earthquakes and volcanic eruptions. The resulting gap that is created is called a rift valley when it occurs on land and a mid-ocean rift when it occurs in the ocean.

Faults and Earthquakes

Faults are areas where the land is unstable because tectonic plates are moving past each other in opposite directions. The grinding of the rocky edges of the plates against each other causes frequent earthquakes in these areas. The San Andreas Fault in California is an example of such a fault, and it is responsible for the frequent earthquakes in Southern California. These edges that grind past each other are called transform margins.

Earthquakes happen because of stress caused by friction that occurs as the rocks on the edges of the plates rub against each other. When the stress becomes too great for the material at the edges to contain, it is released as energy, much the same way that a stretched rubber band snaps back when released. The material of the lower crust and mantle is elastic and stretches, but the material of the upper crust fractures (breaks up).

The uplifted blocks on the right in the foreground and on the left in the distance show the shifts that have taken place due to earthquakes in the San Andreas Fault (*inset*).

Foreland and Hinterland

Foreland basins are depressions formed during tectonic plate collisions between the point of collision and a mountain. When two continental plates collide and one overrides the other, a depression is formed in the foreland (the lower plate), and a mountain is formed in the hinterland (the upper plate). Frequently, the foreland basin fills up with water. The result is the formation of a sea between the two plates.

Experts believe that this is how the Adriatic Sea was formed. The basin the foreland forms gradually fills with sediment (particles of rock) as the hinterland mountains erode. When the basin is completely filled, it forms a flat plain. At the same time, the mountains erode away into low hills and eventually disappear. Some examples of foreland basins are the Persian Gulf, the Tigris and Euphrates river valley in Iraq, and California's Central Valley.

Types of Mountain Ranges

Mountain ranges are not all the same. Geologists divide ranges into various types based on how they were formed. The following are some common types of mountain ranges.

Folded Mountains

These types of ranges consist of a series of alternating long ridges and valleys (low-lying areas). Folded mountain ranges are created when tectonic plates collide, pushing up land and folding it. Many major mountain chains are folded mountain ranges, including the Alps and the Appalachian Mountains.

Volcanic

Volcanic ranges usually form around boundaries where tectonic plates come together. At these points, the joining plates often create a subduction zone. In a subduction zone, one plate slides under the other, and the lower plate is pressed into the mantle. At the point where the plates separate, hot material from the mantle erupts, forming a mountain. An example of a volcanic mountain range is the Cascade Range, which extends from California through Oregon, Washington State, and British Columbia. Mount Saint Helens, which erupted in 1980, is part of the Cascade Range.

Fault Block

Fault activity raises and lowers land around mountains. A fault block mountain range is created when a geologic fault causes chunks of land to rise up from a valley or causes land between mountains to fall down. An example of a fault block mountain range is the Basin and Range Province in the western United States and Mexico.

Domed Mountains

Domed mountains form when molten rock pushes up through the earth's crust, forcing up the rock above it. The molten rock forms a domed shape. Over time, the molten rock hardens. When the rock that was pushed up erodes away, the domed rock underneath is exposed. An example of a domed mountain range is the Black Hills of South Dakota.

The ground near the dormant Three Sisters volcanoes in Oregon's Cascade Mountains has risen 4 inches (10 cm) since 1996, indicating there is underground magma flowing into the area.

Plateau Uplift

Plateau uplifts are formed by the same process as folded mountains. In this case, however, large areas of flat-topped land are pushed up. This creates a plateau, a large flat-topped area of land that is raised significantly above sea level. An example of a plateau uplift is the Colorado Plateau.

Remaking Mountains

Mountains don't vanish, however. A process called isostatic rebound eventually rebuilds them. Remember that mountains were originally created because two tectonic plates collided. In

the process, one plate slid under the other one, forcing up the upper plate to create the mountains. Those mountains put large amounts of pressure on the lower plate, forcing it down into the mantle. When the mountains erode away, that pressure is

The ranks of hills receding toward the Catskill Mountains were formed by the collision of the North American Plate and the continental crust.

released, and the lower plate rebounds—much like a sapling that you pull down and then release. This isostatic rebound forces sediments from the foreland basin back up to form new mountains. For example, during the Paleozoic era, a piece of the continental crust collided with the North American Plate and pushed up and over it. The result was the formation of vast mountains along what is now the East Coast of the United States and the formation of a foreland basin in the area now occupied by the Appalachian Mountains.

Over millions of years, the mountains eroded away, filling in the basin. The isostatic rebound caused those sediments to form present-day mountains in the Appalachian range, such as the Catskill Mountains. Every time new mountains are created, their composition is different from that of the previous mountains because different sediments go into making them. This is an important fact for identifying the age of mountains.

THE RISE OF MOUNTAINS

Orogeny is a Greek word meaning "mountain generating." The term "orogeny" was first used to describe mountain building by two Swiss geologists, Amanz Gressly (1814–1865) in 1840 and Jules Thurmann (1804–1855) in 1854.

Orogenies are periods of mountain building. We learn about the different periods of mountain building by studying orogens, or orogenic belts. Orogens are the remains of ancient mountain ranges. They are long, thin trails of rocks, with an identifiable structure, that remain after the majority of the mountain above them has been eroded away. Orogens form terranes, blocks of deformed rocks that have broken off one tectonic plate and stuck to another. The orogens have a geological structure that is different from that of the main plate.

The place where the orogen attaches to the tectonic plate is usually a type of fault called a thrust fault. Thrust faults are a type of convergent fault in which two tectonic plates rub against each other, and the edge of the lower plate is thrust up and into the higher plate. When the higher plate is thrust up by the contact, the result is the creation of a mountain range. The Alps, Appalachians, and Himalayas

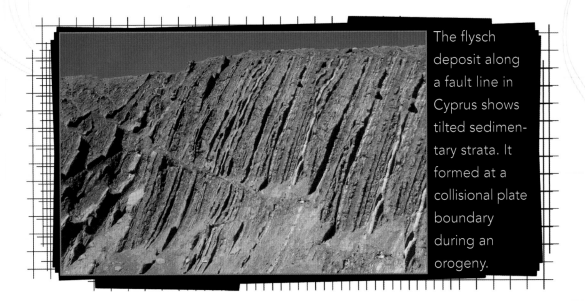

The flysch deposit along a fault line in Cyprus shows tilted sedimentary strata. It formed at a collisional plate boundary during an orogeny.

were formed by such action, which results in the folding and stacking of the land. Such thrusting action means that in some locations, layers of older rock can be found above young rock. As described earlier, mountains all eventually erode. Therefore, there are no existing mountains that date back to very early periods in the earth's evolution. The creation of orogens traps old rock (left over from old, mostly eroded mountains) in younger mountains. Scientists can then study the orogens to learn about the composition of mountains that existed prior to the creation of present mountain ranges.

Gustav Steinmann (1856–1929) was the director of the geological-paleontology institutes at the University of Freiburg in Breisburg and Bonn. (Paleontology is the study of life in previous geologic periods.) In 1906, Steinmann identified several different types of orogenic belts. In particular, he studied the Alpine-type orogenic belt. This type of formation contains:

- Flysch, which is sedimentary rock buried in foreland at the base of mountains that were once under the ocean
- Sandstones, shales, and conglomerate (mixed) deposits of rock that, again, are found in the foreland of mountains
- Ophiolite, which is oceanic crust that has been thrust up into continental crust
- Nappes, which are sheetlike structures of rock that have been folded back on each other when landmasses collide and produce mountains

Stages of Mountain Building

It can take millions of years to build up mountains. The most recent model of mountain building developed by scientists consists of several stages. First, tectonic plates collide. This causes the upthrusting of the earth's crust as one plate is driven under the other plate. The lower plate is often pressed down into the mantle. Eventually, an increase in temperature or a lessening of pressure causes isostatic rebound in which the material in the mantle expands back up. This isostatic rebound also causes the crust to break into blocks, which shift vertically. This process is called fault blocking. Finally, erosion and weathering start to wear away the material of the mountains. All these processes affect the shape of mountains, which changes, or evolves, over time.

Volcanic Mountains

Not all mountains develop as a result of the collision of tectonic plates. Some mountains develop as a result of volcanic eruptions. Volcanic eruptions occur when rock in the crust breaks up as the

MAJOR VOLCANOES

The following is a list of some of the world's most famous volcanoes.

- **Mount Mazama** Located in Oregon, this is the volcano responsible for the formation of Crater Lake around 5677 CE.
- **Mount Vesuvius** Located in Italy, this is the volcano that buried the city of Pompeii in 79 CE.
- **Ojos del Salado (22,608 ft, 6,962 m)** Located in the Andes on the Argentina-Chile border, this is the highest volcano in the world. It last erupted around 700 CE.
- **Mount Fuji (12,388 ft, 3,776 m)** Located west of Tokyo, Japan, this volcano last erupted in 1707–1708.
- **Tambora (9,350 ft, 2850 m)** Located in Indonesia, this volcano last erupted in 1815.
- **Llullaillaco (22,057 ft, 6,723 m)** Located on the Chile-Argentina border, this is the second-highest active volcano in the world. It last erupted in 1877.
- **Krakatoa (2,667 ft, 813 m)** Located in Indonesia between the islands of Java and Sumatra, it last erupted in 1883.
- **Mt. Pelée (4,582 ft, 1,397 m)** Located on the island of Martinique in the Caribbean, this volcano last erupted in 1902.
- **Mount Saint Helens (8,365 ft, 2,550 m)** Located about 95 miles (153 km) south of Seattle, Washington, this volcano last erupted in 1980. Its summit was 1,300 ft (400 m) higher prior to the eruption.
- **Mauna Loa (13,680 ft, 4,170 m)** Located in Hawaii, this is the largest active volcano in the world in terms of overall size. It last erupted in 1984.

result of the movement of tectonic plates. This rupture, or break, in the crust allows molten rock, ash, and hot gas to erupt, or explode, upward. The process by which material is brought up above the crust is called extrusion. Extrusion of lava from volcanoes is one way that mountains are created. The molten rock that spews from volcanoes comes from the mantle. Because the pressure is greater in the mantle, once the rock of the crust fractures, the molten material hurtles up through the opening to the surface. The major component of lava, liquefied rock, is basalt.

Not all volcanoes occur as a result of ruptures in tectonic plates, however. In some places, the earth's crust is stretched until it is very thin. Volcanoes can then erupt through it. Such locations include the Rio Grande Rift in western North America and Africa's Rift Valley.

Another way in which volcanoes are formed is from magma plumes. Magma plumes are columns of hot material that form in the mantle and rise up toward the crust. Because they are so hot, they melt the crust, and then the hot material shoots out into the open. The point where this activity occurs is called a hotspot. Often, the activity in such a hotspot will come to a stop, and the volcano will become dormant (inactive). However, at a future time, a new plume may form and cause another volcanic eruption. For that reason, a dormant volcano remains a threat. A dormant volcano can erupt again. A volcano that is unlikely to ever erupt again is said to be extinct.

Several types of material erupt from volcanoes: lava, pyroclastic material, blocks, bombs, and ash. Lava is magma that flows to the surface, cools, and becomes solid. The term "pyroclastic" comes from the Greek words for "fire" and "broken in pieces." It refers

The summit of the Unzen volcano in Japan was photographed by the Shimabara Earthquake and Volcano Observatory.

to all the solid material that spews out of volcanoes. Often, many small pieces of rock erupt out of volcanoes along with lava and ash. Blocks are solid rocks, whereas bombs are rocks that are still molten inside. Ash is very fine particles of burnt material.

The Pacific Plate's "Ring of Fire" is the most active area of volcanoes in the world. The Ring of Fire is a semicircular 24,855-mile (40,000-km) belt of volcanoes that encircles the basin of the Pacific Ocean. It contains more than 450 volcanoes, which make up 75 percent of the world's active and dormant volcanoes.

Volcanoes don't just exist on land. There are many undersea volcanoes. More than two thousand such undersea volcanoes have been found, ranging from 3,000 to 10,000 feet (915 to 3,050 m) in height.

Types of Volcanic Mountains

The combination of material that erupts from a volcano and the force with which it erupts determine the shape of the volcanic mountain. When most people think of a volcano, they usually imagine a steep-sided mountain with a crater at the peak, created when hot lava and gas erupted. That type of volcano is called a stratovolcano. Mount Saint Helens and Mount Fuji are examples of stratovolcanoes. About 60 percent of the volcanoes on the earth are stratovolcanoes.

Another common type is the shield volcano. This type of volcano looks like a broad shield. Shield volcanoes result from eruptions that produce mainly lava. Since lava is liquid and flows until it cools, the result is a lower, broader volcano. Mauna Loa in Hawaii is a shield volcano.

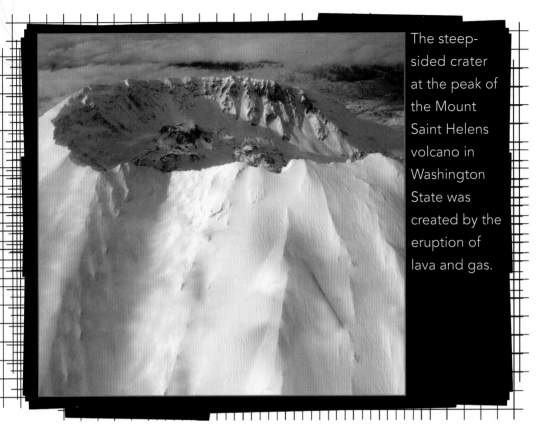

The steep-sided crater at the peak of the Mount Saint Helens volcano in Washington State was created by the eruption of lava and gas.

Another type of volcano is a caldera. A caldera occurs when the most explosive volcanoes erupt. The force of the eruption is so great that it causes the volcano to collapse in on itself, rather than shooting out material that piles up.

THE CHANGING MOUNTAINS

As with everything else, mountains change over time. Some of the changes that take place are the result of natural forces. Others are the result of human actions. Natural forces wear down mountains over time. This process is called weathering. There are two types of weathering: mechanical and chemical. Mechanical weathering is wear and tear that breaks rock down into particles. Wind can scour mountains, blowing away loose rock. In areas where it is cold enough for water to freeze, water can seep into cracks in the mountain. When the water freezes, it expands, cracking the rock around it and causing pieces to break away.

When contact with other material wears mountains down, it is called erosion. Water from mountain streams and rivers wears down rock. Another type of erosion is caused by glaciers, large sheets of ice that form in high altitudes and cold parts of the world. During periods when temperatures warm up, the ice sheets begin to melt and start to slide. As they move down mountains, they pick up debris like rocks and boulders. As they drag this debris with them, they carve away some of the rock they pass over. Weathering is an important process. It produces soil in which plants can grow; it

Limestone is often weathered by the repeated freezing and thawing of water along the planes in the rock. Eventually, the rock is weakened and pieces fall off.

produces aluminum, iron, and copper ore; and it generates sand, gravel, and clay, which are used by people for many purposes.

Chemical weathering occurs when materials in water or air interact with material in rock, causing chemical changes. Some chemical weathering is the result of natural forces. For example, water can interact with minerals in rock, causing the minerals to break down, or decompose. When water causes a chemical change in minerals, it is called hydrolysis. For example, feldspar is a mineral commonly found in rocks. Water from rain, springs, or melting snow can combine with carbon dioxide from the air or soil. When this happens, carbonic acid forms. When this carbonic acid comes in contact with feldspar, it breaks it down into clay. Water that seeps through soil can become more acidic because when bacteria in the soil break down plant and animal remains, the process produces acidic compounds.

Another type of chemical weathering is oxidation. Oxidation occurs when oxygen from the air or water combines with a mineral in rock. Thus, iron often combines with oxygen to produce iron oxide, the compound that is better known as rust.

A third type of chemical weathering is dissolution. This is the simple dissolving of a mineral in water. This is what happens when table salt is placed in water. It breaks down into its basic elements: sodium and chloride. But salt is not the only mineral that dissolves. Some types of rocks are composed of other easily dissolved minerals. This is especially true of certain rocks that are composed of elements that include carbon dioxide. Such rocks are called carbonate rocks. Two such easily dissolved carbonate rocks are calcite and dolomite.

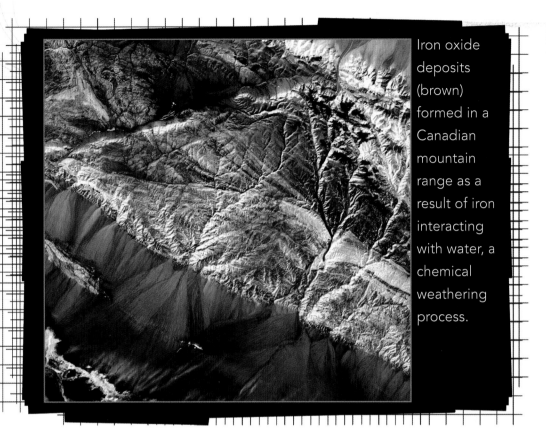

Iron oxide deposits (brown) formed in a Canadian mountain range as a result of iron interacting with water, a chemical weathering process.

Factors That Affect Weathering

First and foremost, the composition of rock affects how easily it weathers or erodes. Rock that is hard and resistant to chemical weathering is less easily eroded than softer rock or rock that easily dissolves.

However, other factors also affect weathering. As discussed earlier, mountain ranges are formed in numerous ways. Mountains that form a smooth, continuous mass, such as lava-based volcanoes, are likely to have less rock flake away than

Mountains like these in Patagonia are weathered by glaciers, large sheets of ice that move over their surface.

mountains composed primarily of thin layers of stacked rock, such as slate-based mountains. Mountains with steep slopes weather faster because gravity easily pulls loose rock down.

Climate also plays an important role. Mountains in areas that get a great deal of rainfall and those in hot, humid climates have a greater amount of chemical weathering because of the greater exposure to water.

Plants and animals play a role in erosion as well. Usage by animals or people can increase erosion. People frequently using mountains in recreational areas for hiking, climbing, skiing, and other activities can cause wear. Even animals that live in the mountains can increase erosion. Burrowing animals in particular can have an effect. In addition to direct wear, animals affect erosion by eating local plants.

Vegetation that grows on mountains holds rock and sediment in place. When vegetation is removed from a mountain, stone and sediment are more easily washed away. Thus, large populations of animals eating mountain vegetation can increase erosion in that area. This is not just true of native animals; large amounts of cattle grazing in mountain ranges can remove significant amounts of vegetation. The more animals there are in an area, the more they are likely to affect the environment. (The same is true of people.)

Human-Related Changes

How people use mountains can affect the rate of erosion. The biggest threat to mountains is not recreational use, but industrial use. Activities like logging remove large numbers of trees that hold rock and sediment in place. Mining directly removes large

MODERN MOUNTAIN DWELLERS: PEOPLE, PLANTS, AND ANIMALS

Mountain ecosystems all contain climates, terrain, and vegetation that change frequently over short distances because of variation in elevation and composition within mountain ranges. Around the world, mountains are home to several thousand different groups of people, such as the Quechua people who live in the Andes of South America.

Nearly forty million people live in the Himalayas, including people of Indian, Nepalese, Tibetan, and Chinese ancestry. However, the lives of many of these people are being disrupted today as a result of the development of mountainous regions for mining and logging.

People who live in high mountains often undergo bodily changes that make them better able to survive. For instance, because the atmosphere is thinner at very high elevations, the number of red bloods cells increases in people who live there. This enables their blood to carry more oxygen at one time.

Mountain habitats provide homes for thousands of plant and animal species. Plants and animals vary from range to range because mountains exist in a wide expanse of environments. Alpine, or high mountains, contain mainly coniferous (evergreen) trees like firs and pines, as well as lichens and wildflowers. They also contain many succulents—plants whose leaves can hold water—because such areas are often dry. They are inhabited by animals like grouse; mountain goats and ibex (wild goats); red squirrels; Steller's jays; hoary marmots; yaks; mountain lions; and Clark's nutcrackers, a bird named after nineteenth-century explorer William Clark. Lower mountain ranges are inhabited by the same types of plants and animals found in non-mountainous versions of the type of terrain they contain, such as forest, grasslands, or desert.

amounts of rock. Direct contact, though, is not the only way that people affect mountains.

The beginning of this chapter discussed natural chemical weathering. However, some chemical weathering is the result of chemicals that human beings put into the air and water. For instance, we produce pollutants like nitrogen oxide and nitric acid when we burn fossil fuels to make energy and run vehicles. The buildup of these chemicals in the atmosphere can result in acid rain. Acid rain occurs when rain or snow combines with acidic compounds from pollutants in the atmosphere. Acid rain can dissolve rock just like naturally occurring acidic compounds in water. However, the additional pollutants we put into the environment can cause mountains to wear down faster than they ordinarily would from exposure to natural compounds alone. Another way in which we affect mountains through the pollutants we produce is through global warming.

Effects of Global Warming

One of the ways in which people affect the environment is through global warming. As the human population has grown and become more industrialized, we have produced more pollutants that affect the atmosphere. Among these pollutants are gases like carbon dioxide and nitrous oxide, which are referred to as greenhouse gases. In an unpolluted atmosphere, sunlight strikes the earth, bounces off, and disperses into space. When greenhouse gases are present in the atmosphere, they reflect the sunlight that bounces off the earth back down to the surface. This causes an increase in temperature, which affects many aspects of the climate and environment. This is called global warming.

Pollution from industry in large countries poses a threat not just to living things but to non-living ones as well, such as mountains.

One effect that global warming has on mountains is causing glaciers to melt faster. Glaciers are large sheets of ice frequently located in mountains. Studies have shown that from the 1850s to the present, the rate of glacial melting has increased. Glacial melting has led to flooding that has drowned mountain villages, and the collapse of glaciers has destroyed mountain towns. However, glacial melting is not the only effect of global warming on mountains.

In some places in the Alps, scientists have found that perma-frost (ground that is always frozen) has melted. This has led to the crumbling of some parts of mountains, causing the land to sink under buildings. Such glacial changes increase the erosion of mountains, as well as disrupting the surrounding area.

As with many areas of our environment, it is up to us to protect mountains from the adverse effects of our activities.

GLOSSARY

asthenosphere The lower mantle.

biostratigraphy Using the fossilized remains of plants and animals to date geologic strata.

continental crust The part of the earth's crust that is on land.

converge Come together.

decompose Break down into basic elements.

dormant Inactive.

erupt Explode upward.

evolve Develop over time.

extrusion The pushing up of material from the mantle to a point above the level of the earth's crust.

fossils The remains of prehistoric plants and animals that have turned to stone.

fracture Break up or crack.

geochronology The technique of directly dating geologic strata using high-tech instruments.

glacier A thick sheet of ice.

gradient A steady increase or decrease.

hydrolysis Chemical changes in rock brought about by contact with water.

lava Liquid melted rock that flows from a volcano.

lithification The process by which sediment is compacted into rocks.

lithosphere The earth's crust and upper mantle.

lithostratigraphy The study of the changes from one stratum to another.

magma Molten rock in the earth's mantle.

magma plume A column of hot material from the mantle that erupts vertically.

magnetostigraphy A technique for studying the direction of the earth's magnetic field at different times by measuring metal particles in strata.

mantle The part of the earth between the crust and the core.

metamorphosis A change in the nature of a material; for example, the changing of limestone to marble.

meteorite A rock from outer space that hits the earth.

meteorologist Scientist who studies climate.

orogeny A period of mountain building.

paleontology The study of life in earlier geologic periods.

rupture A break in a surface.

sea level The average level of the sea between high and low tide.

sediment Tiny particles of rocks worn away from mountains by erosion.

strata Layers of rock; a single layer is called a stratum.

subduction The act of one tectonic plate sinking beneath another tectonic plate.

terrane A block of rock that breaks off one tectonic plate and sticks to another.

FOR MORE INFORMATION

Canadian Geophysical Union
Department of Geoscience, University of Calgary
ES 278, 2700 University Drive NW
Calgary, AB T2N 1N4
Canada
(403) 220-2794
Web site: http://www.cgu-ugc.ca
The Canadian Geophysical Union sponsors an annual prize for the best student paper on geoscience.

Geological Association of Canada
Department of Earth Sciences
Room ER4063, Alexander Murray Building
Memorial University of Newfoundland
St. John's, NL A1B 3X5
Canada
(709) 737-2532
Web site: http://www.gac.ca
This organization provides geological fact sheets and special student programs for college students.

Geological Society of America
3300 Penrose Avenue
Boulder, CO 80301

(303) 357-1000

Web site: http://www.geosociety.org

The Geological Society of America offers educational programs, CDs, articles, and books on geoscience.

History of Earth Sciences Society

c/o Dr. Emma C. Rainforth

Theoretical and Applied Science

Ramapo College of New Jersey

505 Ramapo Valley Road

Mahwah, NJ 07430

(201) 684-7209

Web site: http://shop.historyearthscience.org

This group offers a student subscription to *Earth Science History* magazine.

International Union of Geological Sciences

c/o Dr. Peter T. Bobrowsky

Geological Survey of Canada

601 Booth Street

Ottawa, ON K1A 0E8

Canada

(613) 9470333

Web site: http://www.iugs.org

This organization hosts the Young Earth Sciences Conference for young people interested in geology.

Sierra Club

85 Second Street, 2nd Floor

San Francisco, CA 94105

(415) 977-5500

Web site: http://www.sierraclub.org

The Sierra Club provides a variety of information and activities related to protecting the environment and mountaineering.

U.S. Geological Survey

USGS National Center

12201 Sunrise Valley Drive

Reston, VA 20192

(703) 608-4000

Web site: http://www.usgs.gov

The USGS is devoted to the physical environment and provides news, tutorials, and publications on many of the topics covered in this book.

Web Sites

Due to the changing nature of Internet links, Rosen Publishing has developed an online list of Web sites related to the subject of this book. This site is updated regularly. Please use this link to access the list:

http://www.rosenlinks.com/lan/moun

FOR FURTHER READING

Alshire, Peter. *Mountains*. New York, NY: Chelsea House, 2008.

Bjornerud, Marcia. *Reading the Rocks: The Autobiography of the Earth*. Jackson, TN: Basic Books, 2006.

Clifford, Tim. *Geology*. Vero Beach, FL: Rourke Publishing, 2008.

Davis, Barbara J. *Earth's Core and Crust*. Strongsville, OH: Gareth Stevens Publishing, 2007.

National Geographic Society. *Earth Science: Geology, the Environment, and the Universe*. New York, NY: McGraw-Hill, 2003.

Reed, Christina. *Earth Science Decade by Decade*. New York, NY: Facts On File, 2008.

Stille, Darlene R. *Erosion: How Land Forms, How It Changes*. Mankato, MN: Compass Point Books, 2005.

Thompson, David. *Processes That Shape Earth*. New York, NY: Chelsea House, 2008.

Trumbauer, Lisa. *To the Core: Earth's Structure*. Chicago, IL: Raintree, 2006.

Winchester, Simon. *Krakatoa: The Day the World Exploded, August 27, 1883*. New York, NY: HarperCollins, 2003.

BIBLIOGRAPHY

Barnes-Svarney, Patricia, and Thomas E. Svarney. *The Geology Answer Book*. Detroit, MI: Visible Ink Press, 2004.

Fortey, Richard. *Earth: An Intimate History*. New York, NY: Knopf, 2004.

Hamblin, W. Kenneth, and Eric H. Christiansen. *Earth's Dynamic Systems*. Englewood Cliffs, NJ: Prentice Hall, 2003.

Lambert, David, and the Diagram Group. *The Field Guide to Geology*. New York, NY: Facts On File, 2007.

Murck, Barbara. *Geology*. Hoboken, NJ: John Wiley, 2001.

Pidwirny, Michael. *Fundamentals of Physical Geography, eBook*. PhysicalGeography.net, University of British Columbia. Retrieved August 16, 2008 (http://www.physicalgeography.net/fundamentals/10k.html).

Rosenberg, Gary D. "Nicholas Steno's Chaos and the Shaping of Evolutionary Thought in the Scientific Revolution." *Geology*, Vol. 34, No. 9, September 2006, pp. 793–796.

Than, Ker. "Taller Mountains Blamed on Global Warming, Too." Live Science, August 4, 2006. Retrieved August 16, 2008 (http://www.livescience.com/environment/060804_mountains_growing.html).

INDEX

About the Author

Jeri Freedman earned a B.A. degree from Harvard University. For more than a decade, she worked for companies producing scientific equipment and performing environmental testing. Among the numerous books she has written for young adults are *The Human Population and the Nitrogen Cycle*; *The Rising Seas*; *Genetically Modified Food*; *Applications and Limitations of Taxonomy in Classification of Organisms: An Anthology of Current Thought*; and *The Grassland Biomes: Prairies, Steppes, Savannas, and Pampas*.

Photo Credits